Kids on Board

Kids on Board

Fun Things to Do While Commuting or Road Tripping with Children

Robyn Freedman Spizman

TV's "Super Mom"

FAIRVIEW PRESS   MINNEAPOLIS

Published by Fairview Press, 2450 Riverside Avenue South, Minneapolis, MN 55454.

Library of Congress Cataloging-in-Publication Data
Spizman, Robyn Freedman
      Kids on board: fun things to do while commuting or road tripping
    with children / Robyn Freedman Spizman.
        p.   cm.
    ISBN 1-57749-025-8 (pbk. : alk. paper)
    1. Games for travelers. 2. Family recreation. 3. Automobile travel.
    I. Title.
GV1206.S68   1997
794--dc21
                                  97-2962
                                      CIP

First Printing: April 1997

Printed in the United States of America
01 00 99 98 97   7 6 5 4 3 2 1

Cover design: Richard Rossiter

Publisher's Note: Fairview Press publishes books and other materials related to the subjects of social and family issues. Its publications, including *Kids on Board,* do not necessarily reflect the philosophy of Fairview Hospital and Healthcare Services or their treatment programs.

For a free current catalog of Fairview Press titles, please call this toll-free number: 1-800-544-8207.

Dedication

"But I have promises to keep
and miles to go before I sleep."

—Robert Frost

To all parents who dedicate themselves daily to their kids on board, and to my own loving parents, Phyllis and Jack Freedman, who set the best example ever for being parents. To my wonderful husband Willy for his unwavering support and love, and to our children, Justin and Ali, who continue to teach us how to make every mile count!

Acknowledgments

My warmest thanks goes to my publisher, Edward A. Wedman; Dan Verdick and Jessica Thoreson, who helped this book reach its final destination; all the wonderful individuals at Fairview Press who believed in my ideas; and my editor, Robyn Hansen, to whom I am very grateful. To Genie and Doug Freedman; Dr. Sam Spizman; Gus Spizman; my beloved grandmother, Pauline Blonder; dedicated aunt, Frances Ritchkin; and all my fabulous family and incredible friends for their encouragement. A special thanks also goes to the multi-talented Marla Shavin for her wonderful suggestions, and to Naomi and Adam for road-testing them. To Bettye Storne and Jennifer Frye for cheering me on to the finish line, and to Drs. Marianne and Stephen Garber, Janet Glass, Jill Becker, Steve Aveson, Tracy Green, Meredith Bernstein, and H. Jackson Brown, Jr. for their support.

Other Books by Robyn Freedman Spizman

A Hero in Every Heart (with H. Jackson Brown, Jr., author of *Life's Little Instruction Book*)

When Words Matter Most

The Thank You Book

Lollipop Grapes and Clothespin Critters

Good Behavior (with Drs. Stephen and Marianne Garber)

Beyond Ritalin: Helping Your ADD/Hyperactive Child (with Drs. Stephen and Marianne Garber)

Monsters under the Bed (with Drs. Stephen and Marianne Garber)

The Bad Day Book (with Tracy Green)

The Great Big Bulletin Board Book

If Your Child is Hyperactive, Inattentive, Distractable: Helping the ADHD Child (with Drs. Stephen and Marianne Garber)

Table of Contents

Introduction

If you're a busy parent, going in a hundred directions daily and feeling like half your life is experienced in a car, then you've arrived at the right place. *Kids on Board* is not just another entertaining book filled with fun things to do—it's the Minivan Generation's guide to making the most of every mile with kids on board. With today's hectic schedules, finding time to spend with our kids has become difficult. But help has arrived! Spending valuable time with your kids doesn't have to take a back seat to other demands. In fact, now more than ever, car time can be quality time.

Kids on Board presents hundreds of fun things to do while commuting or road tripping with your child, but it's also a way to make the most of the valuable time you have. Everybody has a chance to build great memories daily and make a difference in their child's life, and the car is one place where you certainly have a captive audience. So go for it! Try a song or two, laugh, teach your child something new, or just enjoy the benefits of a relaxed child who enjoys talking up a storm. Not only does everyone get along better and learn skills for entertaining themselves, but the kids won't drive you crazy when they're distracted with constructive things to do or think about. Best of all, you and your child can build a special bond through your time spent together.

As a consumer expert on NBC affiliate WXIA TV's "Noonday" in Atlanta, Georgia, I have presented hundreds of segments on entertaining and traveling with kids. Somewhere along the line, I earned the title "Super Mom." This certainly doesn't mean I'm some superwoman with all the answers! Instead it means I'm always searching for great ideas that really work . . . real solutions for real parents and real kids. I believe it takes an endless supply of creative ideas to be an effective parent, and when you enjoy the process, the journey is much more rewarding. For the past fifteen years, I have shared the resources I've discovered with others, hoping to ease the job of parenthood. Making the most of the time you have with your kids will be something you'll never regret. As parents, we all strive to do a super job, and the good news is that we get new chances to succeed every day.

So, if the kids in your car keep asking "Are we there yet?", put this book into full gear. These ideas have been road-tested and kid-approved, but you should search for perfect matches for the kids riding in your car. Find out what the kids are studying in school, and choose games that reinforce those skills. Look to your children for new ideas and old favorites. Choose a few games a week to try out and play with your children and passengers, and don't feel overwhelmed by all the choices. One idea will become a family or carpool favorite, and before you know it, you will have mastered most of the games and activities. Most of them are designed for short car rides (twenty to thirty minutes). They can last as long as the ride does, or just as long as they're fun. The length of a game will depend on the length of your ride, the number of kids in the car, the kids' ages and attention spans, and so on.

**This symbol means that you will need to bring
something along to play the game.**

There's also an alphabetical index of game names in the back. I think you'll find *Kids on Board* appropriate for kids of all ages, not just the younger ones. Whether you are a Soccer Mom on the go or just getting started on your carpooling or commuting journey, take a deep breath and treasure the time and the kids you have on board!

One

Are We There Yet?

Easy Rider: Beginning Tips for Triumphant Trips

"Are we there yet? How far do we have to go? I'm tired of sitting in the car. This ride is taking forever. I'm hungry. When are we going to be there? I'm bored. Are we there yet?"

Comments like these are familiar to anyone who has traveled with a child. No matter how old children are, once they're in the car, they all want to know, "Are we there yet?" Children naturally have a hard time sitting still, and car rides seem to last forever. As an adult, it's easy to forget that point of view. However, there are positive things you can do to teach a child how to travel in a car successfully, even when it feels like the ride will never end. If car time

1

becomes quality time, the children in your car will soon discover the benefits of the ride. From cooperation to observation to being able to tell "when they'll get there," this chapter has tips for making the ride an easy one.

First things first! Every child who enters your car should know what you expect. You must be clear and consistent with them, from buckling in to climbing out. Pretend for a moment that when you bought your car a set of rules came with it for being a good passenger. Even better, declare your rules—print them on an index card and keep them in the car so everyone can see them.

Here are some rules that have worked for our carpools over the years:

- Buckle up as soon as you get in the car.

- Keep your hands and feet to yourself.

- Use an "inside" voice and speak nicely to each other. No secrets, name calling, or unkind words.

- Do not distract the driver.

- Do not get out of the car until it has come to a complete stop and the driver says it's time.

- Remember to say thank you for the ride!

For years I kept a silk sunflower in the corner of my dashboard as a simple reminder to the children to say thank you when the ride ended. If someone forgot to say thank you, all I had to do was ask them if the sun was shining or if they had seen any flowers that day. Saying thank you makes everyone feel good and encourages positive behaviors that will be carried from car to car.

Encouraging a Peaceful Ride

Cooperation in the car is essential for safe driving. Sitting still, staying quiet, and getting along can be big tasks for some children, and young ones often need time to learn these skills. These activities will build your children's car skills and increase their (and your!) ability to enjoy car rides.

Car Stars

Play a game with your passengers that helps them learn the idea of "quiet on the set." Pretend you are filming a movie about a carpool, and they are the car stars. Let the children talk and then, each time you say "quiet on the set," have them be perfectly silent. Eventually, the kids will grow accustomed to being quiet—and perhaps quieting down will become something fun to do!

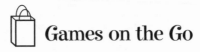 # Games on the Go

Keep everyone happy and occupied minute by minute by bringing along a stash of toys in your car. Fill a bag with small, safe, age-appropriate toys that can be passed from child to child. Divide your trip in half and allow the children to play with one toy at the start of the trip, then switch toys halfway through. This will help keep your children constructively entertained and encourage an awareness of distance measured in relation to how long it takes to play with their toys.

Baby on Board?

Infants on board present a special challenge when traveling or riding in the car, and require a great deal of preparation and attention. Some games are perfect for babies, and a child is never too young to learn how to play! Interacting with your infant is a positive experience for the whole family and strengthens family bonds. Through play, even small children can learn to be creative and interact with others.

Is There an Echo in the Car?

Talking to your baby as you drive along is a great thing to do. To encourage a response from your infant, whenever your baby makes a cooing sound, repeat the sound he or she makes. Then try your hand at it. Make the alphabet sounds, and before you know it, your little one will be echoing your every word.

Nature Nurture

Since my children were very young, we have loved watching a favorite tree in the neighborhood change colors throughout the seasons. We call our tree the Fire Tree because in the fall, it turns brilliant shades of orange and red. Adopt a tree or a plant in your travels, and give it a name. Encourage your child to look up what type of tree it is when they get home, and stop each year to take a photograph of your child standing next to the tree. As the tree grows, so will your child, and these memories will be valued forever.

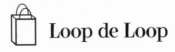 # Loop de Loop

Bring along two dozen paper strips and some tape. As the children in your car cooperate, give them each a paper strip and encourage them to make a paper chain by connecting the strips. The goal of the ride is to make the chain as long as possible. In the beginning, you could reward the children with a paper strip for just five minutes of cooperation, then work toward longer time periods. Each child could be in charge of taping his or her strip to the next one to create the chain. Making the chain could become an ongoing game— the chain would grow longer ride by ride, and your carpoolers might be rewarded with a piece of it if they cooperate for the entire trip.

Kid of the Day

Here's a game that is especially helpful when your carpool gets a little rowdy. Create an imaginary badge that is awarded to one or more of your passengers each trip for being a super kid and a terrific traveler. At the end of the ride, name the kid on board who deserves the title. This game, which focuses on the positive, helps reinforce good behavior. Over time, every passenger should have a chance to be "kid of the day." If everyone behaves, make it a tie!

Developing Observation Skills

A child's environment is filled with stimulating resources, and the children in your car will benefit from you teaching them to see the world around them. These games will challenge your children to observe their surroundings and find a ton of fun as you roll along.

Spot

Encourage children's involvement in the ride by introducing them to the world around them. "Spot" will help you accomplish this. After pointing out details from your neighborhood, challenge the children to spot who lives or works in their area. From the mailman, the crossing guard, or the toll booth collector to delivery people and drivers of familiar cars and trucks, everyone has a different job, and these folks often enjoy waving to kids on the go. Once a child spots someone he or she knows by name or can identify by occupation, the child scores a spot. The more spots, the better!

Measuring Time and Distance

"We're almost there," is a parent's motto when driving. Even though it seems like you're minutes away, a child's experience is very different. These games will give your children methods of measuring time and distance in ways they can understand.

Just a Minute

Teach your child the concept of a minute—kids have trouble understanding how long sixty seconds really is. Say "go" and have the children guess when a minute is up. Put one child in charge of the watch or car clock and make him or her the timekeeper. The kids will soon become experts at estimating time.

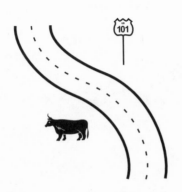

Measure the Miles

A mile might sound like a long way, but it's really not that far. Choose a route you regularly take, like to school or the grocery store. Set your mileage clock and tell the children as you drive when you reach a half mile, a mile, etc. Have the children choose a landmark that marks each point to remind them how far they've come. A particular telephone pole or street sign might indicate a half mile, and so on. Once they begin to recognize landmarks on a familiar route, they'll know how far they still have to go.

Count the Blocks

This game is great for a trip you take often on roads made up of blocks. First, explain to your child that a block starts at one curb and ends at another, and there is usually a street separating each block. Next, instruct your child to begin counting how many blocks you pass to get to a particular place. A trip to the ice cream store might be sixteen blocks. Have your child figure out when you are halfway there. Eventually, he or she will navigate your trip block by block and give you a report of how many blocks are left until you reach your destination.

High Five

Here's a game to help your child measure distance. The start of your trip begins at your little finger. When you arrive at your thumb, you're there. So when your child asks, "Are we there yet?" just answer, "We're at your ring finger." When you're almost there, say that you're at the pointer finger. Of course, when you arrive, everyone gives the driver a high five.

 **The Chain Game**

While at home, have your child make a paper chain with thirty paper loops. Bring the chain along in the car to measure the length of a trip. Each loop can represent as many minutes as you'd like. With younger children, each loop might be a minute. As a minute passes, the child removes a loop from the chain. Older children can remove one loop after five minutes have passed. At the end of the ride, your child can tell you how long the ride was by counting the number of loops removed from the chain.

Two

The A to Z of Fun, Fun, Fun

Fun and Games with the Alphabet

Ready, get set . . . here comes the good old alphabet! This chapter is packed with quick and easy alphabet games and activities suitable for all ages. Alphabet games are no mess, simple to do, and everyone has to put on their thinking caps for them to work. These games will take your passengers for an exciting ride from A to Z!

11

Alphabetical Carpool

This is a game for the first child who gets in the car. Have him or her state each carpooler's first name, including yours, in alphabetical order. As each passenger gets in, the names must be rearranged alphabetically. The game continues until all the names have been stated in the correct alphabetical order.

When I Grow Up

Challenge players to think of as many careers as they can that begin with each letter of the alphabet. From artists to baseball players to carpenters, everyone gets a turn trying to think of a career that begins with the letter that pops up next. The object of the game is to keep going until you reach Z. Some letters are harder than others, but encourage the children on board to look at businesses you pass or people you see as you are driving, and be aware of all the careers around us. From police officers to farmers to bus drivers, careers can be found everywhere we look.

Silly Sentences

Create a silly sentence using words that all begin with the same letter of the alphabet. Each player in the car gets a turn, and the object of this game is to see who can make the longest sentence. Applaud everyone's efforts, and let each child give it a try with different alphabet letters. Some examples include:

Alice ate apples, although apricots are abundant and also available.

Beautiful Betty bought bright blue bags.

Alphabet Names

Have each child take his or her first name through the alphabet, making it rhyme. I would start by saying my name, Robyn, then repeat it beginning with each letter of the alphabet: Robyn, Aobyn, Bobyn, Cobyn, Dobyn, etc. Some alphabet letters present a challenge! Count how many real names come out of this game, and be sure to have the children let you know which names were their favorites— besides their own, of course.

Alphabet Monsters

This game is especially appropriate for younger kids. Use the letters of the alphabet to bring to life a family of wild and wacky monsters. Someone begins by giving his or her alphabet monster a first name beginning with A and a last name that starts with the word "Monster" and rhymes with the first name. For example, A is for Alexander Monsterander, B is for Betty Monstereddy, C is for Clyde Monsteride, D is for David Monsteravid. The game continues until you reach the letter Z.

Alphabetical Favorites

Here's your chance to share your favorite things, from things you like to do or eat to things you like to play with. The first person says, "My favorite thing is . . . ," then states a favorite thing beginning with A, such as an apple. The next person says the first favorite thing, then adds his or her own favorite thing beginning with the letter B, and so on: "My favorite things are apples and baseballs. . . . " Each person gets a turn at listing favorite things. The game goes on and on until everyone in the car can't remember who said what or what comes next.

Gimme Five!

This activity is great for older children who love a challenge. Choose five alphabet letters in a row, such as ABCDE or DEFGH, then create a sentence using words starting with those letters in the right order. For example, a sentence for ABCDE might be "A baby can't do everything." For an added challenge, construct a sentence that describes a career you'd like to have when you grow up, or any career at all. This game is tough, but thinking minds will appreciate the chance to try it. Here are some more examples:

ABCDE: A Brilliant Creative Dedicated Educator

ABCDE: A Bright Corporate Determined Economist

DEFGH: Dependable Excellent Friendly Gorgeous Homemaker

 **Tree ABC**

Have children name trees and flowers in alphabetical order, from apple to zinnia. Which plants grow in your neighborhood? Bring along a plant guide and have kids identify the plants they see.

Knock, Knock

This game will encourage everyone to think of all the people they know—class members, friends, or family members. The first player says, "Knock, knock," and a second player says "Who's there?" The first player answers with a name beginning with A and adds something about that person, like, "It's Ali and Ali loves gymnastics." The second player then says, "Knock, knock," and the game continues with a name beginning with B, such as "It's Betty and Betty has a dog." Everyone has a chance to play, but the object of the game is to encourage the children to really think about the people they name and consider something special about that person.

I Love You More Than . . .

Here's a meaningful game that is perfect to play when it's just you and your children in the car. Begin the activity with the letter A by saying, "I love you more than the fastest airplane." Then your child chooses something that begins with the next letter and says, "I love you more than the tallest building." The game continues down the alphabet, and the object is to get really silly with all your "I love yous." Before you know it, you'll be saying, "I love you more than the fluffiest cloud or loudest dragon."

Mismatch Batch

Encourage your passengers to name two words that both begin with the letter A and absolutely do not match. For example, A is for animals and artichokes. The words must have nothing at all in common. Players then take turns continuing down the alphabet, making sure nothing matches. B is for baseball and bananas. What starts with C?

State It

This game is a tried-and-true winner for kids who are learning about cities and states. Anyone in the car can start this game by saying a city or state that begins with the letter A. Everyone in the car gets to identify whether the place they say is a city or state and if it's a city, what state it is in. For example, the first player would begin with "A is for Atlanta." Then someone would respond, "That's a city in the state of Georgia." The next player would say, "B is for Buffalo," and anyone in the car could jump in to say, "That's a city in the state of New York." The game could continue until you've gone through the alphabet or gone around the country!

A to Z, What Do You See?

This game encourages every passenger to search for things that begin with each letter of the alphabet in order. Begin with A and start your search. From animals to buses to cars, anything goes.

Atlas Alphabet

Ask the first child to name a place that might be on a map, like "Georgia." The second child then names a place that starts with the last letter of the first word, like "Arkansas." The next child would name a place that starts with S. Suggest that kids take place names from road signs, and give them an atlas or a city map if they need more help. For older kids, play this game using only city names or only state names. To add more difficulty, have kids give a fun fact for each of the places they name. The first child might say, "Atlanta is a city in Georgia." The second child could add, "My grandma lives in Arkansas." Kids who play this game will pay close attention to their geography lessons!

The Other Side of the Road

Here's a terrific alphabet game for two children. Assign each child one side of the road. Taking turns, challenge them to find things on their side that begin with each letter of the alphabet, starting with A and working through to Z. For example, A is for animals. The other player finds something that starts with B (a billboard, for example). For added fun, time how long the game lasts, and encourage the duo to break their record the next time they play.

Acura to Zephyr

Try naming types of cars that begin with each letter of the alphabet. Everyone could take turns, or just jump in when they have an answer. The letter A might be for Accord, B for Bronco, C for Chevrolet or Chrysler, and so on. For a more difficult variation (better for kids old enough to read), try spotting these cars on the road. But remember, you can't use a car out of order!

A-Day

Give the children in your car something special to look forward to! Each time you drive, choose a different letter of the alphabet. One day it's A and the next day it's B. On the assigned days, have your passengers search for things that begin with that letter. Kids will be surprised at how many objects they spot beginning with that letter when challenged to look carefully.

Who's Who?

Beginning with the first letter of the alphabet, challenge the children in your car to name famous people from all walks of life. From Albert Einstein to Aristotle, this game has endless opportunities. A fun spin on this game includes having the children name what the person was famous for.

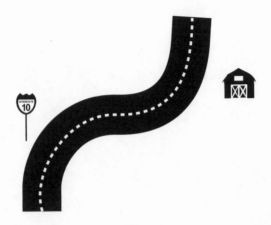

Shop Till You Drop

Tell the children in your car that you are going on a shopping trip and they must describe everything you will put in your shopping cart. Begin the game by having one child at a time say any letter of the alphabet. Taking turns, each player in the car must say something that begins with that letter. For example, if one child says the letter C, then the other children might say carrots, candy, cantaloupe, and cashews. The object of the game is to see how many items they can think of that begin with that letter. An extra challenge is to specify a certain kind of store—a grocery store or a clothing store—and to limit the list to items found there. You'll soon understand the phrase "Shop till you drop"!

Snap and Clap

This activity involves the entire carpool in a fun way. Assign a specific sound or movement to each of three alphabet letters. For example, if you say the letter A, the kids must snap their fingers. If you say the letter B, they must clap their hands. And if you say the letter C, the children must make kissing sounds. Begin playing by saying each letter slowly, then speed up the game for added fun.

Alphabet Soup

Start with the letter A and have each passenger name a vegetable to put in your alphabet soup. The first round from A to Z could be real vegetables, then tell the kids they can add some fun ingredients like aardvarks and bugs! You're bound to get some really wacky responses with this recipe.

ABC Sentences

Encourage the children to create a sentence by stringing together words in alphabetical order. You can either work together as a group, or older kids could have a contest to see who can get the longest sentences. Here's one of our best: Aunt Betty called dear Elaine for good housekeeping information just knowing lazy Mary needed our pots . . . (help!). If you keep getting stuck in the same spot, try starting somewhere in the middle of the alphabet for variety.

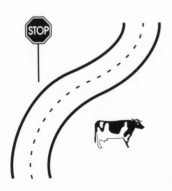

Jump Rope on Wheels

Remember the jump-rope song that featured Alice and Andy who came from Arkansas and sold apples? Why not have your carpool make up a jump-rope song using their favorite characters from books?

Some examples are:

C—my name is Cinderella and my husband's name is Charming and we visited China and we saw chopsticks

B—my name is Big Bird and my friend's name is Bert and we come from Busytown and we sell bananas

Backwards Alphabet

Here's a challenge for all your passengers. Each child gets a turn to try to say the alphabet backwards. Beginning with Z, state each letter from Z to A. The object of this game is to be able to say the backwards alphabet really fast.

Rhyme Time

Have the children choose a word and try to rhyme it in alphabetical order. For example, if you choose the word Are, then you would say, "Bar, Car, Dar." As soon as a player says a word that does not exist, the rest of your passengers must say "BOP!" which rhymes with "stop" and means "we caught you!" Once a player is bopped, it's the next player's turn. Players can start with any word beginning with any letter, but they must continue the alphabet in order from that letter as they rhyme their words. Go ahead and try it: Book, Cook, Dook (BOP!). Care, Dare, Eare (BOP!) Fill, Gill, Hill, Ill, Jill, Kill, Lill (BOP!). Let, Met, Net, Oet (BOP!).

Ice Cream Alphabet

Challenge your passengers to create an ice cream alphabet. Starting with A and ending at Z, each child gets a turn and must name a flavor of ice cream. Can't think of any? Make up new flavors as you go! Here are some examples of flavors my carpool came up with: A is for apple pie a la mode, B is for banana banana, C is for chocolate mountain, D is for double fudge nut, and E is for everybody loves vanilla. Once the kids get the scoop on playing this game, they're bound to beg for more.

Doubles and Triples

Here's a game that isn't easy, so your passengers will have to keep their eyes on the ball . . . or should I say license plate! Instruct the children to search for license plates that include double or triple alphabet letters, such as BB or CCC. Whenever they see a set of matching letters, they score a point per letter. This game can also be played by searching for three consecutive alphabet letters in a license plate combination, such as ABC469 or DEF380.

The Longest Word

What's the longest word you can think of that begins with A? Pose this question to your carpool and see who can think of the word with the greatest number of letters. A might be antidisestablishmentarianism. Next try B, and so on. Count the letters of each word and see who comes up with the longest word. Whoever wins scores a point, and although the rider with the most points wins the game, everyone wins by learning new words.

ABC TV

Play ABC TV by naming television shows, new or old, that begin with each letter of the alphabet in order. Here are some examples: A is for *All in the Family*, B is for *Barney*, C is for *Chicago Hope*, D is for *Davy Crockett*, and so on.

ABC Stoplight

This game is perfect for trips that include a lot of traffic lights. Every stoplight you pass under scores a letter. Begin with the letter A and see how far down the alphabet you get. Your passengers can take turns by going in alphabetical order of their first name. The object of this game is to see if you can travel all the way to Z in one trip. Kids who remember a familiar route might know it's an M or P trip, helping them with their measurement of distances. And, if you take a new turn, the game has a new twist!

Cartoon Alphabet

Encourage your kids to think of their favorite cartoon characters, and using the alphabet letters in order, see how many characters you can name. Passengers can take turns or this can be the carpool challenge of the century. Here are some of our favorites: A is for Archie, B is for Barney, C is for Casper, and D is for Dino.

Alpha-Blast

Here's a game that's out of this world! Encourage your passengers to pretend they are going to the moon. The players must each name objects that they would take to the moon, beginning with the alphabet letters in order. When it's their turn, they must begin by repeating what the previous person said. For example, "I'm going to the moon and I'm taking an apple." The next player says, "I'm going to the moon and I'm taking an apple and a book." The game continues until no one can remember all the items going to the moon.

Side by Side

This game is great to challenge traveling minds. Encourage the children to think of two letters of the alphabet that are side by side and also stand for the initials in a person's name. It can be any person, including themselves, you, someone famous, a friend, or a family member. For example, RS is Robyn Spizman, EF is Ella Fitzgerald. This game is hard, but you'll be surprised at the number of answers they come up with.

ABC Deeds

Encourage kindness by playing this game. Have each child think of a good deed that starts with each letter of the alphabet. Next car ride, see how many of your ABC deeds your players actually did. Here are some of our suggestions:

A—Always say please and thank you.

B—Bring back a library book when it is due.

C—Call Mom if you're running late.

D—Don't use the last bit of milk without
telling Mom or Dad.

ABC Zoo

Challenge your passengers to name an animal for every letter of the alphabet. Begin with the letter A and in alphabetical order give each player a turn. Here are some ideas to help you get started: A is for anteater, B is for baboon, C is for cat, D is for dog, E is for elephant, F is for frog . . . have fun!

 Three

Carpet Rides and Private Eyes
Using Your Imagination

One thing that all children always have with them is their imagination. Challenging children's imagination teaches them to solve problems, create exciting solutions, and ultimately entertain themselves. The following games are open-ended and have limitless possibilities for fun. Whether you are creating a dream, riding a magic carpet, or saying goodnight to the objects in your room, your passengers are bound to love putting their imaginations to work.

Goodnight Room

Here's a game to play with one or more children. Ask the children to picture their room and all the objects in it. Then have them pretend they are going to sleep, and that you must say goodnight to everything in their room. Each child gets a turn saying goodnight to his or her room. If you have a full car, you might let each child say goodnight to five things at a time.

Time Flies

Time flies when you're having fun, so put those little ones' minds to work and decide what would happen if time really could fly. Pretend you had a remote control unit that operated time. Give each child a turn to tell you what he or she would slow down, fast forward, and stop. To when would they go if they could go backward in time? To when would they go forward?

 Rulebook Rally

Do the kids in your carpool play soccer, tennis, or other sports? Keep a rulebook handy and quiz them (or have them quiz each other) on the rules of their sport. Start questions with "What happens if . . . ."

New Rules

What would happen if football players wore swimming suits? Have kids change the rules on the games they know. What would happen if these new rules were the real rules? Have kids give reasons why it is important to have rules.

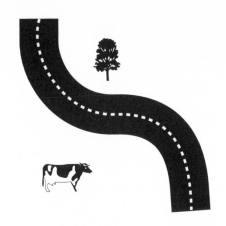

Six Degrees to Ketchup

Every food can be connected to ketchup in no more than six steps. Choose a food to start, like buns. Buns go with hamburgers, which go with fries, and (of course) ketchup. Be careful, because this game can make you hungry . . . .

Building a Sandwich

Here's a sequencing game for any number of children. Start out with the questions, "What comes first when you're making a sandwich? What comes next? What comes after that?" The children should take turns answering the questions. Then encourage the children to add the secret ingredient—imagination! The children will surprise you with their bright ideas for sandwich making, so be prepared for a few bugs, dinosaurs, a little goop, and anything on earth in their sandwiches.

Cooks on Board

Ask kids what their favorite foods are. Do they know how they are made? Have your passengers guess the ingredients in each of their favorite meals.

My Favorite Things

Each child gets to take turns naming their favorite things. Favorite things might include people, foods, things to do, clothes, toys, and so forth. An added imagination exercise would be to have the children explain why these things are their favorites. Everyone has lots of favorite things, so this game can go around and around until you get to your destination.

Emotions

Talk to your passengers about feelings. (This is a great game if someone is having a "bad day.") What does being happy mean? Being angry? How do you let other people know how you feel? Let kids take turns sharing "happy thoughts" or "scared thoughts" and making faces to show what these feelings are like.

I'm Special Because . . .

Build the children's self-confidence and awareness of their special qualities with this game. Give them turns saying something about themselves that makes them special. Children might be special because they help set the table, they are nice to their baby brother or sister, or they say thank you. The obvious sequel to this game is You're Special Because . . . . Encourage each child to say something positive and truthful about another child in the car. For example, "Ali's special because she helps me buckle my seat belt when I have a hard time."

Paint the Town

In real life, the sky is usually blue, grass is green, and clouds are white. Encourage your passengers to color their world, and think of different colors for things we see every day. How would life be different with a purple sun?

 Boo!

Kids love being scared. Let them scare themselves silly by telling ghost stories. Bring a bag of props to help them along (fake fur, fangs, a mask, etc.), and give each child one to use in his or her part of the story. Make sure each child gets a turn to add to the story.

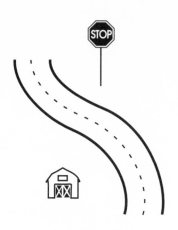

Punch Line

Let each kid make up a punch line, then think of a joke to go with it. To kids, everything is funny!

Pack It Up

Pretend you are all packed up for a special car trip. Let each passenger tell you where they would like to go. To take this trip, however, they must also tell you what city their destination is and any details they know that might help you get there by car. How does their destination differ in appearance from where you are? What does the landscape look like? What is the weather like? As the children improve at this game, challenge them to choose destinations in a different country or across the ocean. How would you get there in a car? What would it be like?

Stargazer

When traveling at night, explain the concept of constellations (and point out any you know). Do they know any constellations? Have kids find their own constellations, name them, and make up stories about them.

Night Light

Play this game when you and your children are traveling at night. Challenge each child to think of all the things that have their lights on. From headlights to lamps to night lights, the list goes on and on. With luck, after they're finished, they'll be ready for lights out!

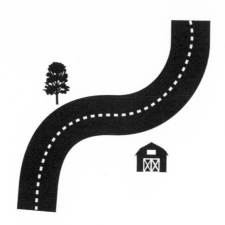

Dream On

Ask your passengers to see if they can remember the silliest dream they ever had. Let the carpool vote on who has the wildest imagination.

Investigative Reporter

Have the children imagine they are television reporters and they have to interview everyone in the car. What might they ask that the world would find interesting? Here are some leading questions:

What is something you have done really well?

**What is the most exciting thing
that ever happened to you?**

What is the hardest thing you've ever done in your life?

What was the best vacation you've ever had?

If

Play a what-if game with your passengers. Each child gets to ask another child "What would you do if . . . ?" Fun "ifs" include:

**What would you do if you
met the President of the United States?**

**What would you do if you
went to the moon?**

A variation of this game is "What would you say if . . . ?"

News Prediction

Have your riders imagine that they could predict the news. This is especially fun when there's an election or something very newsworthy happening. Start out with tomorrow and let each child give a news prediction. See who comes the closest to the real thing, and talk about how they could change lives by knowing what was going to happen ahead of time. What would they do with this extraordinary skill?

Golden Rules

Ask your passengers if they know "the golden rule," which is "Do unto others as you would have them do unto you." What does it mean? Why is it golden? What are their golden rules?

Yuckity Yuck

Here's a game that's totally yucky. Ask each child to think of a sandwich that combines foods that really don't go together. From peanut butter and spaghetti topped with mustard to tuna on rye with sardines and baloney, anything really yucky goes!

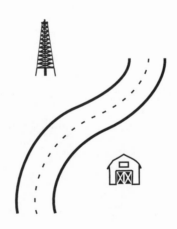

When I Get Home

Ask each passenger what they would do if they could do anything they want when they get home from school. This game is at its best when imaginations are working. At the end of the game, have all the children vote for whose house they would want to visit after school!

Desert Island

Here's an old standby that's always thought provoking. Ask the children, if they were stranded on a desert island and they could only bring two things to eat, what would they be and why? Which two books would they bring and why?

It's a Wrap

Challenge your passengers to name everything they can think of that is wrapped up. This could include baloney, a sandwich, gift, baby in a blanket, and on and on. This game is hard, but you'll be surprised at the possibilities and creative thinking it inspires. When the game ends—it's a wrap!

Tea Time

Here's a fun way to encourage pretending and imaginative thinking. Ask your passengers to pretend that they are having someone famous over for tea. Each child gets a turn and must describe their tea party in detail, saying who is coming, what everyone will be wearing, and what the topics of conversation will be. From the snacks to the party favors, be sure to get the whole scoop.

Best Friends

Ask each child to imagine being best friends with someone famous. Who would it be and why?

Helping Hands

Take a look at what is happening outside your car windows. Have the kids tell you what they see: people, cars, trees, animals, etc. Do they see anyone who needs any help? Is someone raking leaves, shoveling snow, or mowing the lawn? Does someone have a car full of groceries? Have kids think of things they could do to help these people, like bag the leaves or help with the groceries. What other kinds of things could your passengers do to help out?

Shape Search

Here's a game to reinforce your children's knowledge of shapes. As you ride along, ask your passengers to spot shapes in things you pass. For example, a house might be a square with a triangle on it. A restaurant might be a rectangle. Watch for circles, triangles, squares, rectangles, cones, pyramids, ovals, etc.

Big

Challenge your children with this question: If they could make big anything that's small, what would it be? You'll be amazed at their answers and active imaginations! A variation on this game is its opposite—make small something that's big.

Happy Holiday

On the days around a holiday, have kids talk about what the holiday means, how it is important, and how different people celebrate it. Make up songs about the holiday. Bring treats and decorations and have your own car party!

Beach Party

Have your passengers pretend they are going to the beach. Ask each of them what they would pack. Then have them imagine that they are really there, right at the seashore. What would they hear? What would they see? What would they feel?

A Thrill of a Skill

Have your passengers imagine that they could instantly learn to do something. From knowing their multiplication tables to skiing down a mountain, everyone can choose one thing they wish they could learn in an instant. Encourage a car discussion and ask the children why they picked those skills. Discuss how long those skills might take to learn. Whose skill was the most difficult to learn? Whose was the easiest?

 # My Own Map

At home, give kids a pencil and paper and have them draw a map of your route, adding street names and things they see along the way. Bring the map along in the car so your child can compare the homemade map to a "real" map of the city. How are they the same? How are they different?

Blast Off

Tell kids that today's trip will be a ride around the solar system. You will start at Pluto and the destination is the sun. Throughout the ride, talk about each of the planets and have kids say what they know about them.

First Things First

If you're on the road to school, ask your carpoolers about the very first thing they will do once they set foot in their school. Let each child describe what they do first, second, third, etc. They'll have to think carefully about this one and put their best foot forward to remember what they actually do, step by step.

Meet and Greet

Ask the children who they would like to meet if they could meet anyone on earth. Why would they want to meet that person? If they could introduce that person to anyone else, who would that be and why?

Fast Talk

Have the children in the car pretend they've received a phone call from someone very famous. Who would they like it to be? What would they say to them if they had five minutes to talk?

Do You Have a Dream?

On a more serious note, talk with your passengers about Martin Luther King, Jr. He had a very important dream of peace and equality for people of all races and religions. Ask the kids about their dreams and wishes for humankind.

True Friends

Encourage a conversation about what a true friend really is. Ask the kids in your car to imagine the greatest friend on earth. What do real friends do for you? How do they help you? How can the children be true friends to others? Take turns naming things you can do with your friends. Who is your best friend? Why?

A Penny for Your Thoughts

The object of this game is to encourage your passengers to share whatever is on their mind. Pass a penny to one child and say, "Here's a penny for your thoughts!" Everyone should get the chance to speak their mind, and whoever has the penny can choose who goes next.

Back Seat Driver

Start with "If I were driving . . . " and have kids say where they would go and what route they would take, then what would happen once they arrive.

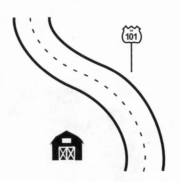

 ## Weather or Not

Make your car a weather station! Keep a notebook for kids to record simple weather information, like temperature, cloud cover, wind speed (windy or not windy), precipitation, and any other details they'd like to add. Have kids "predict" the weather for the afternoon or the next day and write their "forecast" in the notebook. Later, check the forecast to see if the kids were right.

Animal Hitchhiker

What would happen if an ostrich was waiting by the side of the road? Where would it be going? Would it have any luggage? If so, what would it pack? More importantly, how would it fit in the car? Have kids think about all sorts of animals who might need a ride.

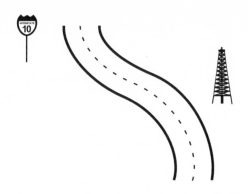

World's Record

Ask your passengers to imagine that they have just set a world's record. All players get a turn describing what their world record would be set in. Encourage them to think beyond athletic contests such as pole vaulting or downhill skiing—stretch their imaginations to world record bullfrog jumping or chili-dog eating!

Look Out Below

Have your passengers imagine that they are the tallest people on earth. Ask them: "How do you think it would feel to be the tallest person on earth? What things would be hard to do? What might be easy to do? How would your life change? What would you have to do differently every morning? What do you think the headlines would say about you?"

Fill in the Blanks

This game should encourage conversation and spark your passengers' imaginations. Ask the children to finish a sentence any way they'd like. Here are some examples:

I have to . . .

I love to . . .

When I grow up I want to be a . . .

The funniest day in my life was . . .

I'll never forget the time . . .

One Wish

If your passengers could each have one wish, what would they wish for? This game can go in many directions, or you can give it a particular theme. For example, you could have gift wishes, earth wishes, edible wishes, etc.

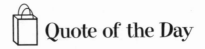 Quote of the Day

Bring along a copy of a quotation book that appeals to you. Every day, recite a quotation to your carpool. Ask your passengers to discuss the quotation. What does it mean? How does it apply to them? Encourage your carpool to search for quotations at home and in school and share them with the rest of the group every time you drive.

And the Story Grows On

The object of this game is to have the group tell a story with each passenger adding a new line. You begin by stating the first sentence in the story. Each passenger adds another sentence, and the story grows on from there. Really imaginative groups could continue stories from day to day. Some great story starters include: "Once upon a time there lived a very big giant," or "I'll never forget the time my family went on a trip."

Future Inventions

Not long ago, it was impossible for people to imagine an electric broom. Talk with your carpoolers about many of the recent advances in technology and science. Challenge them to think of and invent something that does not exist . . . yet, that is! What invention might they create? How would it be an improvement over what already exists? Have your carpoolers vote after all the inventions have been shared, and talk about which inventions might really work. You never know when you might have an Einstein on board!

Lost and Found

Tell your carpoolers to imagine that they just found a lost puppy. The puppy does not have any identification on him, and needs a home. Give each child an opportunity to tell you what kind of puppy it is, what he's like, and what they would do to help him find his owners.

I See, You See

This is a two-player game. The first player says what he or she sees, then the second player says what he or she sees. Players take turns, but cannot name anything that has already been seen. At first this game is very simple, but it gets more difficult as the miles fly by.

Calling All Eggheads

Here's an egg-stra special game that will challenge your passengers to be very inventive. Ask each child to think of a way to roll an egg down the stairs without breaking it. Each child must describe a creative way to wrap and protect the egg so it won't crack or break. Some ideas include wrapping the egg in cotton, then in bubble wrap. Another highly inventive approach involves cutting open a beach-ball, filling it with packing material, putting the egg in the center, then sealing the hole. Now we're on a roll! You'll be surprised at all the creative ideas, and some might even crack you up.

Give a Hand

Encourage the children to create different kinds of animals using their hands and fingers. Finger-friendly creatures include an octopus, a crab, a bunny rabbit, or a kitten with whiskers. Let the children's imaginations roll as they try to suggest animals with their hands. For children sitting next to each other in the car, this is the perfect guessing game.

Pickle Pete

Encourage your passengers to think of silly names that combine real names with food. Some of our real dillies include Banana Bob, Apple Ali, Mango Meredith, and Jelly Jack. Make sure everyone in the car gets in the spirit of the game and chooses a name, and encourage them to think of names for their teachers, friends, and even their pets! For even more fun, ask each passenger to create a rhyme using the silly name.

Pickle Pete
He's really neat
He has juicy news
And cucumber feet.

Ha, Ha, Ha

Challenge your passengers not to laugh while playing this very silly game. The first player says ha, the second player says ha ha, the third player says ha ha ha, and so on. The object of the game is not to laugh, no matter how many ha-has you must say.

President Elect

Ask your carpoolers to imagine that they are the president of their school. Ask them what they would do first. How would they help the school? If they were going to do something silly that the kids would love, what would that be?

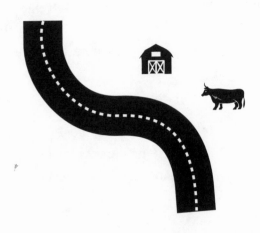

House Names

Have a carpool discussion about whether we look like our names. Does Ali really look like a Jennifer? Ask them to imagine what other names they would have chosen besides their own. Then encourage them to give people's names to houses. Which house looks like a Victoria or a Jeremy? If you're stopped at a light, kids would even have the time to name some cars. Is there a Madge or a Reginald on the road?

Animal, Vegetable, Mineral

Ask the children to imagine that they are vegetables. What type of vegetable would they be and why? What kind of animal, or flower, or bird, or car would they be? This game can prompt some very silly discussions!

Switch-A-Roo

Imagine that everyone in the car switches roles. One child becomes you, you become one of them, etc. Everyone gets a new identity and must play the part. This game is especially fun for little ones who love pretending they are Mommy or Daddy or a big sister or brother.

My Life as a Dog

Encourage your children to imagine what life would be like for them if they were one of their pets. What would it be like to be a dog, or a cat, or a guinea pig . . . or a goldfish? What would they do all day? What would they eat? Would it be boring or exciting? What would make it most different from being a kid?

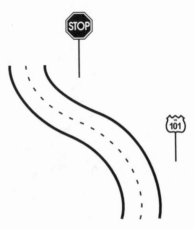

What's Up?

See how many things you can all name that answer the question "What's up?" From birds, airplanes, wind, trees, and lightning, you'll be surprised at how many things are up in the air!

Private Eyes

Pretend you've got a car full of private eyes and they've hit the streets looking to solve a mystery. Ask your passengers to carefully look at something as you drive by—maybe a house you pass every day, or a new shop in the area. After you pass by, ask them about details. What color was the front door? How many windows were upstairs? Was it brick or stucco? Encourage them to examine these things as all good P.I.'s do! Then challenge their imaginations and ask them to tell you a story about the people who live or work there.

Magic Carpet Ride

Ask your passengers to imagine that they could ride anywhere in the world on a magic carpet. Where would they go? Why would they want to go there?

Bon Appetit

Ask your carpoolers to imagine that they are waiters at a fancy ethnic restaurant—it could be French or Italian, for example. Each child must describe the menu to the other passengers. Brainstorm with the children about other foreign destinations where you might dine, too!

 **Baby, Baby**

Little ones love to snuggle up with a favorite stuffed animal or doll while riding in the car, so bring a pretend baby to keep on board. Bundle up the baby on board in a small blanket and give your child a turn taking care of it. If your carpool is filled with young children, this activity can also be played as a game by assigning a big brother or big sister for that day. The big brother or sister can be in charge of teaching the rest of the carpool a lullaby for the baby and also demonstrate safe games the baby would enjoy.

Grab It and Go

Ask your carpoolers to imagine they are the one-thousandth customer at a toy store, and their prize is a shopping spree. However, there's a catch. They only have five minutes to shop. Give all the children a turn to explain what they would do, including describing the items they would grab first. This game is so much fun, you can also try it at the pet shop, the grocery store, the mall, and so on.

All Grown Up

Encourage your passengers to imagine what they would be like if they were all grown up. That's right—an official adult. Give the children turns describing the careers they will have. Where will they live? Will they have families? What will they wear to work? What would they want for their birthdays when they are all grown up?

Shape it Up

Name a shape and challenge the kids on board to name something that has that shape. For example, a line might be a stick. A circle might be a ball. A square might be a present. See how many objects your passengers can name for each shape.

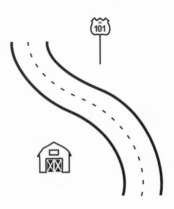

Calling All Cars

Look at the passengers in other cars. Imagine that you can call them on the telephone and ask them three questions. What would you want to know? Have another child answer these questions as someone in another car might.

 Four

On Beyond License Plates
License Plate and Number Games

Ever since cars have been on the road, license plate games have been a family favorite. From learning where people were from to laughing at personalized plates, the fun has grown and grown. While this chapter certainly pays its due respect to license plates, it also offers a new set of ideas for lively math and number games. In addition to being fun, these games will help strengthen children's math skills because many of them reinforce basic math concepts.

Counting Teeth

Here's a game that's a mouthful of fun. Challenge the children to count their teeth with their tongue. Go ahead and try it, it really works! See who has the most teeth, the least teeth, etc. Who thinks they have the biggest teeth, or the smallest? Once each passenger has given a tooth count, see who has an even number or an odd number of teeth.

Repeat After Me

Here's a game that will encourage excellent listening skills. Say a sequence of numbers that are out of order, such as 1, 7, 3, 9. Ask the children to take turns repeating the sequence back to you. Each child who listens carefully and repeats it correctly will score a point. This game gets more complicated and challenging as you add more numbers to the sequence.

Kiss Math

Give your child math problems by using kisses instead of numbers. Instead of saying "One plus two is what?", make a kissing sound for each number. For example, "(kiss) plus (kiss, kiss) is what?" Younger children love this game, and the fun adds up!

Road Sign Addition

Encourage the children to search for road signs that have numbers on them. Then ask them to add up the numbers on the sign. See who can find the sign that adds up to the highest amount.

Number Rhyme

This game is especially fun for younger children who are learning how to rhyme. Say a number, then go around the car to each child to rhyme a word with that number. Keep going until someone can't think of a rhyming word. Then try another number. For example: one, sun, fun, run, ton, done, bun, gun, nun, pun, run, won . . . whew!

Lucky Numbers

Assign each child a number, or let them choose their own. The goal of this game is to find license plates that do not include your number. If your number is two, then any license plate without a two scores you a point. The child with the most points when you reach your destination is the winner.

Three Stump

Give your passengers a category such as ice cream, colors, or sports. Encourage each child to name three different objects or items that fit in that category. The object of the game is to stump the players. No one can repeat anyone else's answer, so the children really have to think to come up with trios.

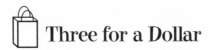 Three for a Dollar

Ask your kids, "If oranges are three for a dollar, how much do I have to pay if I only want one?" Vary the number of items for a dollar (or two dollars), and the number to buy. To make the game more real, bring along grocery store advertisements and have kids figure out how much the specials cost.

Heads Up

Enourage your kids on board to name whose head is on each type of money. From pennies to dollar bills to silver dollars, see if they know who's who and what's what in the world of money.

Add it Up

Here's a game for older kids who are learning addition and money facts. Tell the kids that you have one Abraham Lincoln, a Thomas Jefferson, and a Ben Franklin. Challenge them to add up all the presidents for a grand total. Create different presidental combinations for some monumental fun.

Number Search

Search for things in your environment that resemble numbers. A tree might look like the number one. A stop sign might look like a zero. Before you know it, you'll definitely be seeing things you never saw before!

Did You Ring?

Instruct the children to search for the numerals in their telephone number—in order—on the license plates they see. When they spot the next number of their telephone number, they should say it out loud. The goal is to be the first one to find your entire telephone number. As each child completes the phone numbers, encourage the rest of the children to finish their numbers. See whose telephone number was the most difficult to find, then play this game another day. Compare your results: is one number really more difficult than another, or is it the luck of the draw?

License Plate Plus

Give each child a turn to spot a license plate and see how quickly he or she can add up the numbers. If a license plate was 27A9DF, the child would add up 2 plus 7 plus 9 and say the total as fast as possible . . . 18!

Birthday Bingo

Everyone loves their birthday, and this game focuses on that special day of the year. To begin playing, ask each child to say their birthday in numbers. For example, November 7, 1986, would be 11-7-86. Have the children search for their birthday numbers in order on license plates. Whoever finds their correct numerical birthday first wins, but everyone should have the opportunity to find their birthday.

Oldest to Youngest

Ask each child to think of his or her family, or another if they desire, then name them from oldest to youngest. This game is good for reinforcing sequencing skills in younger children.

Name a Number

This game requires some creative thinking. Name a number for the group, then challenge them to come up with different ways to say that number. For example, the number one could be once, uno, single, solo, etc. Two might be twice, double, deux, duo, twins, pair, etc. The higher you go, the harder the game becomes!

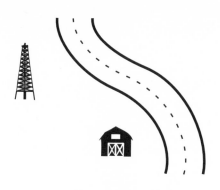

Number Chain

Here's a game that goes on forever—or at least as long as your car ride! Begin by having one carpooler call out a two-digit number. In a round-robin style, each child must name a number beginning with the second digit of the number before. For example, 17, 72, 24, 46, 65, 59, 93, 38 . . . you can create a number chain that doesn't stop!

Two, Four, Six, Eight

This game will have your kids on board really cheering. Use the familiar cheer "Two, four, six, eight, who do we appreciate?" as an example. Encourage each child to finish the cheer with new words, or redo it completely with new numbers. It can be serious or silly, and some of the cheers will really be neat. Here's one that my carpool came up with:

Twos, fours, eights, tens,
School is out and we're all grins.

License 4 Fun

Search for unusual and creative license plates that make statements, such as "I M NOT 4T." R U RED E? Let's go!

Hat Hunt

Here's a game that your riders will love for its limitless possibilities. Each child gets a turn at naming something to search for. These things can be easy to find, like a car with one dog in the back seat or a car with three people in it, one of whom is wearing sunglasses. You can really make this game hard by requiring more and more details, such as a red truck with a driver who is wearing a baseball cap.

Tell-All Telephone

Here's a fun game that kids will love. Ask each child to name a person and his or her telephone number. If a kid can't think of any more numbers, that child is "off the line" and out of the game. Whoever knows the most numbers wins.

Quick Count

Challenge your carpoolers to quickly count up a variety of things: how many people in the car have brown eyes? Blue eyes? Are wearing red? You can also make this game more difficult by asking harder questions like "How many brown eyes are in the car? How many red items?"

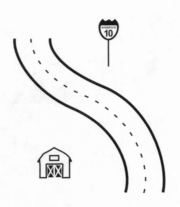

Counting All Cars

Ask the children to choose a particular kind of car or van—a convertible, a four-door car, a station wagon, etc.—and count every one that they see. They score a point for each one, and the winner is the one with the highest score when you reach your destination.

Counting Rhymes

Challenge kids on board to create silly rhymes that incorporate numbers in them. For example:

One, two, three
Look at me
I'm as silly
As can be.

Three, six, eight
I cleaned my plate
I ate my lunch
And it was great!

Conversation Starters

Ask the children in the car to name three things that they did well that day. Then ask them to name two people they played with. Vary the questions and assign specific numbers to each one. You'll be happily surprised at the wonderful answers you hear and all the information you learn. Turn the tables and let the children ask you questions about your day. "Name five places you drove today!"

Mission Initials

Have the children search for license plates containing their initials—or, even more challenging, that start with their initials. Passengers can search for two initials and score two points, or three initials and score three points. The object of the game is to score the most points. Although this game is hard to win, it will keep the children occupied for quite a while.

Who's on First?

Start a carpool tradition and encourage the children to always say "Happy first" on the first day of the month. As the children get in the car, they will have a few minutes to say "Happy first" and show they know what day it is. It's always fun to see who remembers, and it's often a surprise even to the driver that a new month arrived so quickly.

What's the Date?

Everyone forgets what date it is now and then. As each passenger gets in the car, see if the child can tell you the exact date, naming the month, day, and year. After everyone is on board, see how many kids knew the correct date, and reinforce what it is.

Sign Off

As you drive to a specific destination, challenge your carpoolers to count all the signs they see. At the end of the trip, ask one passenger to record the amount. Next time you drive that exact route, try counting the signs again. Did the numbers match? If not, try, try again!

Button Your Shoelace

Here's a silly game to encourage counting skills, especially for younger children. Ask each passenger to count all the buttons they are wearing. Once they have counted their buttons, compare totals and see who has on the most buttons. Then continue this game by having them count all their shoelaces, zippers, snaps, and even their Velcro strips!

All Eyes on Board

Ask your carpoolers to close their eyes and give a total of how many people are in the car. Next ask them to add up how many girls, boys, passengers wearing red, etc., are on board. Think of as many questions as you can that encourage children to either add or estimate a particular number. When their eyes are open, they can check their scores and see if they were right.

Pairing Up

Talk with your carpoolers about things that come in pairs. For example, dice come in pairs, twins come in pairs, and so do shoes. See how many other pairs your passengers can name, and then ask them to search for things as you drive along that also come in pairs.

Addition Attire

Have each child add up the articles of clothing they are wearing. See who has the most items on. Each piece of clothing equals one point. Shoelaces don't count!

License Plate Multiplication

Have the children take turns multiplying the first two numbers of the next license plate they see. This game is especially fun for children learning their multiplication facts, and a great way to reinforce those math skills. One child can even play this game alone as you drive along.

State Plate

Here's a new twist on the license plate game. Each time you spot a license plate, one passenger must name something about that state. For example, when you spot a Georgia license plate, a passenger could say, "Atlanta is the capital of Georgia," or "Georgia is the peach state."

Number Bumble

This game is fun for younger children who are learning their numbers. The child must say, "Number Bumble, I see three," naming a number they see outside. The child must finish with a funny rhyme, such as, "Sitting on my grand-pa's knee." The game continues: "Number Bumble, I see four, running out the kitchen door."

License Plate Pictures

Many license plates have pictures representing something about that state. See how many license plates your passengers can spot that include illustrations on them, then discuss what the pictures represent.

Truck Stop

Next time you're on a busy street or commuting on the highway, challenge the children to search for trucks that have more than one license plate on them. See which truck will hold your car's world record for the most license plates.

Ten Points

The object of this game is to find license plates with numbers that add up to ten. For example, 532-JHW would be a winner, since 5 plus 3 plus 2 equals ten. When passengers find a winning plate, guess what they score? Ten points! Top score wins when the ride is over.

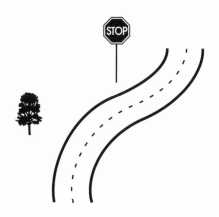

Five

I Spy, Who am I, and Guess What?

Guessing Games

Everyone loves to try their hand at guessing games. The element of surprise makes the ride more enjoyable, and the ability to take a stab at the unknown keeps everyone happily occupied. This chapter suggests games and activities that use guessing as their basis for fun. Guess what? With these ideas on board, your passengers will be miles away from boredom!

Who or What Am I?

Choose a subject—a person or a thing—and encourage your passengers to try to guess who or what you are. Give one clue at a time until someone has guessed your answer. Everyone should have the chance to choose a subject for guessing. Here's an example: I'm black and white and read all over. People love to see me, but are quick to throw me out. I prefer to be recycled. What am I? A newspaper, of course!

Guess Who?

Give clues about a particular child in your car and ask everyone to guess who you are describing. You might say, "This person is wearing a zipper, a smile on their face, and has a spelling book and a blue notebook." Whoever guesses correctly gets to describe the next person for the carpoolers to identify.

Guess the Word

This game begins with each player choosing one word. Once all the words are chosen, turn on the radio. Each time the children hear their word, they score a point. Common words like "the," "you," and "I" are definite winners and bound to be heard easily. The game continues until you arrive at your destination. The player with the most points wins the game.

Telephone Time

When you see a telephone wire, a phone booth, or someone on a cellular phone, give clues about a person who might be talking on the line and ask everyone to guess who you are describing. You might say, "She's your uncle's wife and she's really nice" (Aunt Lois). Or "He visits the house every day but doesn't see us" (the mailman). Whoever guesses the "caller" correctly gets to describe the next person for your passengers to identify. From family members to favorite friends and other people the children know, this game has endless possibilities.

Green Light

Everyone in the car chooses a number from one to nine that they think they will see next. When everyone has their numbers and you are ready to start, say, "green light." The first passenger to spot his or her number scores a point. Keep playing the game until you have arrived at your destination. Whoever has the most points wins the game.

Brainstorming Books

Encourage each child to think of a favorite book and its main character. The other players must guess the name of the book and the character. For example, this character says more than just meow. He lives in a hat. He's lots of fun. Who is it? The Cat in the Hat!

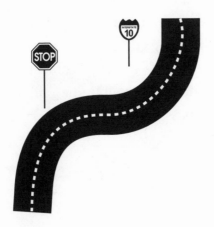

Red, Yellow, Blue . . . I See You

Have each child choose a color. Each time a car of his or her color passes by, that child scores a point. You can make this game even harder by specifying one side of your car. If you say "right," then your passengers only score a point if their color car passes you on the right side.

Pattern Pursuit

Here's a fun game that works best when you are picking up a car full of children. Beginning with the first child in the car, each child gets to guess what pattern of clothing the next child will be wearing that day. Will it be polka dots, stripes, checks, plaid, hearts, teddy bears, or no pattern at all? No one loses at this game, since it's fun to see who's wearing what and who guesses correctly. As each child guesses, the rest of the kids in the car can agree or make their predictions, too.

Family History

Encourage kids to quiz each other about their family history. Ask questions like "Where was your grandma born?" and "Where does your name come from?" Tell your own children stories about their grandparents and great-grandparents, and someday they will pass them on to their kids.

I Spy

Ask each child to predict something he or she will see on the way to your destination. For example, the children might guess that they will see a bicycle, a car, a person, a tree, and a dog. Encourage the entire car to search for these objects and say "I spy" when they spot one. You can make the game harder by looking for things that are more difficult to find, like balloons, two cats, etc.

Colorful Cars

Ask each passenger to make a guess at how many red cars you will see during your trip today. Each child must choose a number, then the entire car counts the red cars as they pass. At the end of the trip, see whose number was closest. This game can change colors daily. By the end of the week, which color car did you see most often? Which was the least seen?

Snack Attack

Have the children think of their favorite snack but not say it out loud. Then have each child describe the snack using sounds they might make when eating it. "Crunch, crunch" might be popcorn! The first person to guess correctly gets to give the next clues.

Animal Talk

Ask your passengers to pretend they are animals that can talk. Have them describe themselves with clues while everyone else guesses what animal they are. For example, a child who chose a lamb might say, "My owner is Mary and I am very soft."

Food Fun

Here's a game the kids on board will really eat up! Ask a passenger to think of a specific food that they really like, but not to say it out loud. The passenger must give clues to everyone else on board about the food, and challenge all players to guess what it is. If it's very sticky, spreads easily in a sandwich, and can be plain or nutty . . . it must be peanut butter!

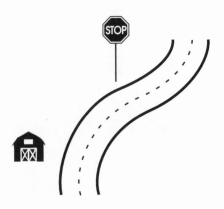

Looking Good

Give everyone in the car about two minutes to take a good look at each other. Then ask all the passengers to close their eyes and, one by one, tell you what another passenger is wearing. Ask them for specific details, such as eye color, glasses, hair ribbons, etc. You'll be surprised to find out what some of them remember . . . and what they forget!

What's Cooking?

This is a game for the children in your car who bring their lunch to school. Ask each child to guess what's in someone else's lunch bag or box. Peanut butter and jelly sandwich? Raisins? Chocolate chip cookies? Juice box? Every item they guess correctly is worth a point.

Super Spy

Here's a fun twist on an old favorite. Ask each child to think of a super spy name that will be his or her secret identification name. Only the carpool will know who's who. Now assign each spy a special mission. When it's their turn, the children must think of something they see as you're driving and keep it secret. The first spy begins by giving a clue to the object, such as "I spy something red." The super spy continues to give hints until someone guesses his or her object.

Guess What?

Here's a variation of the classic Twenty Questions, made easier for younger players. Ask one child to think of an object. The rest of the passengers each get ten yes-or-no questions to try to figure out what the object is. Questions they might ask are: "Is the object an animal? Is it a person? Does it move? Is it small?" Once a child reaches ten questions and can't guess the object or guesses it incorrectly, the next child tries his or her luck. Everyone gets a turn guessing until the object is identified. The game continues with another child choosing an object.

Bubblegum

Have one child think of a verb, such as "eat" or "run," and start the game by saying, "Bubblegum." By using the word "bubblegum," the other children must ask questions to try to discover the chosen verb. Questions might include, "Do you bubblegum at night? Do you bubblegum on your way to school? Do you bubblegum in your sleep?" Once someone guesses the verb, another child can choose one, and the game continues until everyone has had enough "bubblegum."

Timely Guesses

Here's a guessing game that's perfect for a fairly short ride. Give your child an opportunity to guess how long it will take to get to your destination. If more than one child is playing, everyone gets a guess. At the end of the trip, see who was closest to the actual time. You can also play this game by guessing the number of miles to your destination.

I Know a Hero Who . . .

Kids have lots of heroes, from Batman to Mom and Dad. Let passengers guess who these heroes are. One child begins, "I know a hero who . . ." and says some of the things the hero does. The child who guesses correctly gets to choose the next hero.

 ## Paper Bag Presto

Place an object in a paper bag and bring it along with you in the car. The children cannot look inside the bag, but they can try to guess what's in it by shaking it and feeling its shape from the outside. Fun objects are those that don't give themselves away too easily by their shapes, such as a bar of soap or a ball of yarn.

School Biz

Here's a game that reinforces what children are learning at school. Each passenger identifies topics they are currently studying. Then each child gets asked a question relating to that subject. Here are some super questions: How many pennies make up a quarter? How many minutes are in two hours? How many sides are on a rectangle? How many sides are on a dime? How many states are in the United States?

Famous Footsteps

Choose a famous person and have the children guess who it is from your clues. For George Washington, a good clue might be "He never told a lie." While you can get the game rolling, challenge the children to think of their own famous people. They'll love walking in famous footsteps all the way to your destination.

Totally Ridiculous

The first player asks a question like "Do you like artichokes?" The next player must answer the question with a totally unrelated answer, like "Airplanes fly really fast." The next player asks another unrelated question, and the game continues in a round-robin fashion. The object of the game is to ask ridiculous questions and give ridiculous answers that are not related in any way.

What's Cool at School?

Ask each child to think about what's cool about school. At first, some of the children on board might say nothing is cool, but this game will prove them wrong. Ask one of the children, "What's cool at school?" That child should then give a clue to what's cool, such as, "She's in charge of the school and very nice." Any child who guesses the answer might reply, "Mrs. Finkel is cool at school." This game can also be played by simply letting each child say what's cool at school—you'll be surprised at all their answers.

Under the Rug

Tell the children you've hidden something under a rug, then give them clues to help them guess what it is. For example, "I hid a red object under the rug. It has a core. People love to bite it. Sometimes it can be yellow or green." Give one clue at a time until someone guesses the correct answer. That person gets to be next to hide something under the rug. The game continues until there's nothing left to hide or you've reached your destination.

Take a Bite

Tell your carpoolers you've taken a bite out of something, then give one clue at a time until someone guesses the correct food. For example, "It's soft. It's sticky. I eat it in the morning. It's very round." The first player to guess "pancake" goes next. The game continues until everyone has bitten off more than they can chew!

Don't Look Back

Using the fingers on one hand, each player takes a turn and hides a number from one to five behind his or her back. The object of the game is for the other players to guess the number. Whoever guesses correctly scores a point and gets to go next.

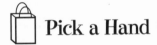 Pick a Hand

Bring a bag with small objects inside. The objects need to fit into the palm of a player's hand and keep hidden when his or her hand is closed—for example, pennies, a small ball, a whistle, or a penny toy. Have one child choose an object and give clues about it to the other children, who must guess which object he or she is holding. When you're filling the bag, be sure to choose objects that are both safe and age appropriate.

 # Mystery Box

This is a wonderful game that might go on for quite a while. Whether you drive once or twice a week or more, the suspense will build as this game continues. Begin by placing a hard-to-guess surprise in a box, then tie the box closed with ribbon. Tell your passengers that whoever guesses what's in the box will get to keep it. Each passenger gets one chance to guess for each ride. The child who guesses correctly wins the mystery box.

 # Magazine Memory

This game encourages a child's observation skills. Open a magazine to a particular page and pass it around the car. Each passenger gets one minute to study the page and try to remember everything that's on it. Close the magazine and go around the car, giving each person a chance to name one thing that was on the page. A wrong guess or no guess puts a player out for that round. The person who remembers the most objects wins the game.

Open and Shut Case

Bring along a magazine to play this guessing game. Begin by having each player choose a word, then ask one child to open the magazine to a particular page, such as page fourteen. Everyone can take turns searching to see if their word appears on that page. Players earn one point every time they find their word. One player might score a lot of points, while others must try again with a different page.

Six

What's the Word, Hummingbird?

Word Games

Words, wonderful words! Long words, short words, hard words, easy words—they come in every shape and size imaginable. This chapter presents a selection of games that use words as a starting point. These games will help build a child's vocabulary while encouraging a relationship with the world of words.

Roy G. Biv

Here's a fun way to teach children the colors of the rainbow. In order, the colors are red, orange, yellow, green, blue, indigo, and violet. If you take the first letter of each of the colors, you get good old ROY G. BIV. Ask if anyone knows Roy G. Biv. Challenge your passengers to guess who he is and what he does. Give the children hints, such as "He's very colorful" and "He comes out only after it rains."

Antenna Banana

Have the children search for car antennas with something attached to them. Every time they see an antenna with something on it, the children must say "Antenna Banana." This game will become a carpool tradition as children search for flags, flowers, or ribbons waving from an antenna.

What's the Word, Hummingbird?

Encourage your carpoolers to make up a variety of clever rhymes. Use these rhymes to say goodbye or hello, or even to initiate a conversation. Be sure to make up some of your own using the children's names. Some examples are:

What's that, Pussycat?

Sit by me, Stephanie

What's new, Kalamazoo?

Days of the Month

Here's a game based on a classic rhyme. Teach your carpoolers the poem about the days of the month:

Thirty days has September,
April, June, and November.
All the rest have thirty-one,
Except February, which has twenty-eight.

Once they've mastered the poem, state a particular month and have the children name the number of days in it.

No Rhyme

Challenge your passengers to choose a word that doesn't rhyme with any other words. For example, the word "blue" has dozens of words that rhyme with it, but try the word "doctor" and you'll probably stump everyone pretty quickly!

Car Parts

Taking turns, have each child name a part of the car. See if kids know the function of the parts they mention. What do they think makes a car go, and why?

The Thank-You Game

This game encourages children's good manners. Go around the car and have each child name someone they owe a thank-you to, and why. Some examples are, "Thank you, Mrs. Estroff, for helping me understand math today," or "Thank you, Dad, for packing me a really great lunch."

Anything Goes

Ask your child to name something that is going up, like an airplane. Then challenge your child to think of something going down, like a skier. Then say "up," then "down," and have your child name something that fits each category. "Up" words include mountain climbing, planets, and air. "Down" words include bicycling, hills, or sky divers. Anything goes . . . as long as it goes in the right direction!

Scrambled Town

Have the kids rearrange letters in names of streets, towns, rivers, and other landmarks to make new names (not all the letters have to be used). For example, Fillmore Street could be Free Lime Store.

Upside Down

Invite your passengers to name everything imaginable that can be upside down. From trapeze artists to upside-down cake to someone doing a handstand, encourage the children to think of as many things as possible.

The Same Game

Say a word and then challenge your carpool to name that word's synonyms, or other words that have the same meaning. For example, "joyful," "glad," and "happy" are all synonyms, and so are "couch," "sofa," and "loveseat."

Homonyms are Happening

Challenge your passengers to identify two homonyms, or words that sound the same but are spelled differently. For example, "piece" and "peace," "wear" and "where," and "bear" and "bare" are all homonyms. Have the children use each word in a sentence that illustrates its correct meaning. See how many they can think of and give them a point for each one that's correct.

Opposites Attract

Say a word and have your carpoolers name that word's antonyms, or words that mean the opposite. For example, "good" and "bad," "up" and "down," and "black" and "white" are all antonyms.

Compound Words

Here's an activity that will compound the fun. Make sure everyone in the car understands that a compound word is made up of two words put together, such as "notebook" or "grandfather." Have someone state a word, then challenge the riders to think of a way to make it a compound word. For example, if the word were "sun," compound words might be "sunbeam," "sunlight," "sunscreen," "Sunday," and so on.

Category Fun

Give your carpoolers a category and ask them to name as many things as they can fit in that category. For example, some categories could be things you play with, dessert foods, or holidays. Depending on the categories, the lists could be endless!

Street Sign Word Search

Here's a challenging game that's good for older children and really superior spellers. As you drive past street signs, have the children read them out loud and search for words within the words on the signs. For example, in the sign "Johnson Road," you can find the word "son" or the name "John." Signs like "Lake Street" may not give you much to work with, but "Gladstone History Center" could be a regular jackpot! Glad, lad, stone, ton, tone, on, one, his, is, story, cent, enter . . . .

Tongue Twister

Create some funny tongue twisters and have each child try and say it five times. Here's one for starters:

**Betty bought bananas because
Bobby begged for blueberries.**

Now, encourage the children to invent some of their own twisters and see who can say them the fastest. Ready, set, go!

Polka-dot Spot

Here's a fun game for little ones. Every time the children spot something polka-dotted, they say the phrase "I spot a polka dot." Pretty soon everyone who plays starts to see spots!

Green Things

This game encourages creative thinking and identification by color. Announce to your carpool that the color of the day is green. Ask them to take turns naming green things throughout the entire ride. Each day you drive, choose a new color and see which color is the hardest or easiest to find, which colors are their favorite, and so on.

Bird's the Word

This game starts with a simple word, any word. The next person has to say a word that has absolutely nothing at all to do with the first word. If the first person says "bird," the second person can say "hollow" or "toothpaste," for example, but not "nest" or "brain." The third person says a word that has nothing to do with the second word, and so on. This is trickier than it sounds! Encourage kids to talk about how words relate to other words, and why some words do (or don't) go together.

Baloney

Each child gets a turn asking a silly question, such as "Are you wearing a green wig?" The object of the game is to answer the questions by saying "Baloney, baloney, baloney" without laughing. Does this game sound silly? (Baloney, baloney, baloney.) This game definitely is ridiculous, but I promise that soon everyone will be rolling along and laughing.

Telephone

In this classic children's game, one child whispers something into another child's ear. This child passes it on, and so on, until the phrase gets back to the first child. The new phrase is usually very different than what the first child said. Why does this happen?

Here, Kitty

Start this game by having one child say "Here, kitty." In a round-robin style, each child must say, "Here, kitty" as many times as it has been said and then add their own "here, kitty." Don't lose count, and try not to laugh when you're calling the kitty!

New Names

Allow everyone in the car to rename themselves. Little ones especially love this game, and they'll be very creative. For that ride only, call each child by his or her new name. When you ask them questions, the children must answer to their new names. This is a great game for building listening skills.

What's in Store?

Ask your riders to pretend they are in charge of renaming all the stores around you. What should they be called? How could their names be improved? For example, a breakfast restaurant might become Pancake Heaven or Hashbrown Town.

Roses and Violets

Ask each child to reword the familiar poem "Roses are red, violets are blue." Here's an example to get you started:

**Roses are sticky,
Violets are best.
I'm so smart,
I got an A on my test.**

Vowel Search

Have the children in your car search for words that begin with vowels. This game will not only reinforce their knowledge of vowels, it will also challenge your carpoolers because many of these words are hard to find.

Backflip

Ask your passengers to search for or say words that make words when they are repeated backwards. For example, the word stop is pots, and spot is tops. This game becomes more difficult when you have to spot the word while driving along. To make it even harder, challenge them to think of words that are the same backwards and forwards. Can't think of any? How about mom and dad!

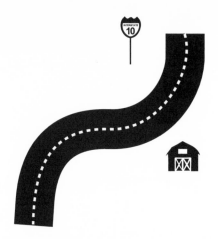

J-Day

Choose an alphabet letter each day and play a word game that focuses on names. Ask passengers to name as many kid's names as they know that start with the letter J. From Jonathan to Jessica, the names will be endless. For an added twist, use animals or foods instead of names.

Big A, Little A

Play a game with your kids on board to reinforce capital and lowercase letters. Challenge each passenger to name a word that begins with a big A, a capital letter. For example, big A is for Alabama and little A is for apple. The game can continue with each child naming words for the next letter of the alphabet.

Double Your Fun

Ask your carpoolers to search the road signs for words with double letters. Give the children a point for each double-letter word they can find. Some words might include street, letter, book, etc.

Compute This!

Play the computer game and challenge your passengers to name words associated with a computer. One passenger might say "disk," the next "keyboard," the next "screen," and so one. Say "delete" to skip a turn. The object is to keep going until no one can think of anything else and everyone says "delete."

Name That Color

Challenge each child to name a color of a crayon. Encourage the children to think of really creative and descriptive names, like ocean blue, candy apple red, etc. Go around the car and give each passenger a turn.

Backwards

See if your carpoolers can introduce themselves and say their names backwards. Once you get the hang of this game, try saying a variety of words backwards and seeing if everyone can guess the words correctly. For example, "Hi, my name is Nybor!" or even, "Ih, ym eman si Nybor!"

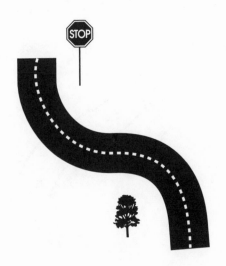

What's the Word?

Challenge your passengers to think of words that have only three letters in them. After the children have listed as many as they can think of, have them try five- or six-letter words, or any other number. Naming different amounts of letters can keep this game going a long time.

Common Grounds

Have a carpool discussion about things each of you have in common. Find out how many of you (including the driver) enjoy playing baseball or eating spaghetti. What other things do you have in common? You'll not only have a lively discussion with the kids on board, but you'll also discover new things that you share with your children and others' as well.

Simile Search

Explain to the kids in your car that a simile describes a resemblance to something—for example, "as blind as a bat" or "as tired as a dog." Ask your passengers to think of as many similes as they can and share them with each other.

Spelling Bee Ready

Conduct a spelling bee on the way to school. The oldest passenger on board can be in charge of giving words, making sure the spelling words are age appropriate. Little ones can even suggest their own words to build confidence. Each player gets a turn, and everyone wins if they learn to spell new words.

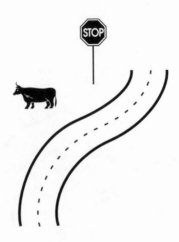

Flip-Flop

This fun word game can last as long as your car ride. The first player begins by saying any word he or she wishes—for example, the word "went." The next player must begin his or her word with the last letter of the word just stated, in this case T. The game continues flip-flopping around the carpool, reinforcing spelling skills as it goes.

Awards on the Go

Ask your passengers to make up awards for people, places, or things you pass on the way to your destination. From the most colorful house to the tiniest dog to the sign missing the most letters, encourage them to be creative with their award giving. You could even have a special award presentation as you drive by and wave!

Tongue Tied

Say a silly sentence or a tongue twister, like "Polly Parrot cooks pot roasts" or "She sells seashells at the seashore." Then ask each child in turn to try to repeat the sentence. See if all the kids can get the phrase right, then let them take turns making up silly sentences to tie the tongues of fellow passengers.

Street Sign Jumble

As you pass street signs, ask the kids to combine pieces of names from several signs. For example, Mt. Vernon Highway and Old Powers Place could become Old Vernon Place or Mt. Powers Highway. This game is also perfect for initiating a conversation about how streets might have gotten their names. Where did the name come from? Is it famous? A variation of this game can be played with signs from businesses. From Aunt Ella's Tackle Shop to Fisherman Joe's Sewing Goods, you can get some pretty unusual combinations!

The Name Game

This game uses your passengers' names in a sentence that rhymes. Some examples are:

Take a hike, Mike.
You're a pal, Al.
I think you're silly, Willy.
Get a job, Rob.
Earn some money, Sonny.
You're great, Kate.

See how many rhymes the children can think of, and encourage them to use their friends' and family members' names as well.

Relatively Speaking

Begin this game by choosing one word and keeping it a secret. Tell your carpoolers five words that are related to your word in some way, then encourage them to guess what your word is. If your word was "candy," your clue words might be "chocolate, peppermint, sticky, gooey, and sweet." The first player to guess your word gets to choose the next word.

Birds on the Brain

See how many different kinds of birds the kids in your car can name. Give each passenger a turn and see how many miles you can go before they run out of bird names. Just think . . . your carpool might know four miles of birds!

Word of the Week

Here's a game that will build your children's vocabulary. Each day, or each week, a different child is in charge of choosing a word to teach everyone in the car. The children should try to choose words that no one in the car knows, then have everyone use the new words in sentences. By the end of the year, your carpool's vocabulary will definitely be improved.

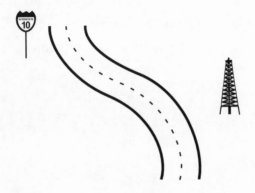

Sentence Scramble

Start this game by saying a complete sentence to your carpoolers. The next player takes the last letter of the last word in the sentence and begins a new sentence with it. The object of the game is to carry on a conversation that makes sense. This is one game with possibilities that could go on for miles. Here's an example: Guess what I'm doing today? You are probably going to the library. You're right! Tomorrow, I'm going to the library, too. Oh no, I think I lost my library card.

On the Move

Tell your carpoolers it's moving day. In round-robin style, each child chooses a place and adds it to the list of what came before. For example, the first person could say, "I'm moving to Dallas." The next person would say, "I'm moving to Dallas and then Hawaii." The next person would say, "I'm moving to Dallas and then Hawaii and then Cleveland." A challenging variation of this game is to think of moving destinations in alphabetical order: Atlanta, Barcelona, Canada . . . .

Positively Speaking

Ask your children to name all the positive words they can and then use them in sentences. Positive words might include optimistic, happy, upbeat, appreciate, enthusiastic, and so on. After they've identified lots of words, encourage your passengers to use one of the words to give someone a compliment.

Initially Yours

Each carpooler can use his or her own initials to create some silly names, funny foods, or interesting pastimes. Here are some of our favorite examples: Justin Spizman, whose initials are JS, loves to eat jelly sandwiches, and his favorite hobby is juggling scarves. Robyn Spizman, whose initials are RS, loves to eat radish souffle, and her favorite hobby is reading stories.

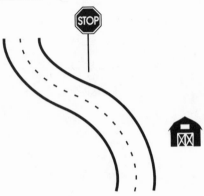

One Thing

A fun activity at the end of the day is to ask the children in your car to teach you something new that they learned that day. Each passenger gets a turn, but they can only name one thing. Just think of all the things you will have learned from each other by the end of the school year!

Seven

Do-Re-Mi and You

Musical Activities

Whether you prefer Mozart or the Rolling Stones, music is a special addition when riding with kids on board. Finding a happy musical median can help everyone enjoy the ride. Even if you just start out playing music you like and music they like, with luck you will find music you both will enjoy together. All it takes is a little time and patience.

Sharing music with our children in the car has been an enlightening experience for us. With kids on board, you have a captive audience and an exciting opportunity to introduce them to a variety of musical styles. Like the teacher in the movie *Mr. Holland's Opus,* you can bridge the generation gap and share your love of music. Before you know it, if you make the most of music while driving, your little ones will be guessing which concerto is which and naming lead singers and drummers in favorite bands. From The Beatles to Beethoven, the following activities and games will definitely make music and the ride more enjoyable!

 ## And the Band Plays On

Teaching kids about teamwork is an important lesson, and sports aren't the only way to illustrate this. A symphony orchestra is another wonderful example of how people "play" together. Purchase a cassette tape of *Peter and the Wolf,* or check one out from your local library. *Peter and the Wolf* has different instruments representing individual characters in the story, and when all the sounds blend together, the story can be told without a single word. Have your riders guess which instrument is which character. Encourage a conversation about how the members of the orchestra must work together. What role does the conductor play? What would happen if no one listened to him? How does teamwork in music relate to teamwork in sports?

Name That Tune

Here's a familiar favorite. Either make a tape of some favorite children's songs or purchase a tape that's totally instrumental. Play the music and encourage the kids to guess which song is which. Whoever guesses the right name scores a point.

Play it Again

Ask each child to name a favorite song. Challenge the children to say all the words, then sing it. Everyone can help keep the words coming.

139

Do-Re Listen to Mi!

Here's a fun way to add a little music to the conversations on board. Whatever each passenger says during a designated time period, he or she must sing it! Each child chooses a song, and must sing whatever they say to the tune of their selected song.

Old MacDonald Had an Alphabet

Here's a fun activity that everyone will love to try. Instruct each child to sing the letters of the alphabet to the tune of a favorite song, such as "Old MacDonald." Your passengers will love this musical activity and enjoy singing their own version of the alphabet song.

The Love Bug

With your kids on board, brainstorm about songs that include the word "love." See how many your crew can name and sing. When you're all sung out, turn on the radio and listen for more songs that include the word love.

 ## Play Misty for Me

Brainstorm with your passengers about songs for stormy weather. Make a tape of those songs to play whenever it rains, in honor of the wet weather. Your passengers will look forward to the rainy-day music, and it will brighten up their day and the ride. A few rainy-day songs to get you started are "Rain, Rain, Go Away" and "Raindrops Keep Falling on my Head."

Sunny Skies

Brainstorm about music that focuses on sunny skies. Give each child in your car a turn to name a song with the word "sun" in it. From "You Are My Sunshine" to "The Itsy Bitsy Spider" to "Here Comes the Sun," the object of the game is to keep going until you run out of bright ideas.

Sound Machine

Making goofy noises is something kids love. Give them a song to sing, like "Happy Birthday," but don't let them use any words, only sounds. Giggles galore!

What's Missing?

While you're listening to songs on the radio or on tape, challenge your passengers to guess which instruments are missing from the songs. Start out with easy questions: Do they hear tubas? Violins? Electric guitars? As time goes on, your passengers will become more familiar with the sounds of individual instruments.

Animal Chorus

Create a sound for each letter of the alphabet, and figure out what real—or imaginary—creature might make it. Then sing the alphabet song using these animal voices.

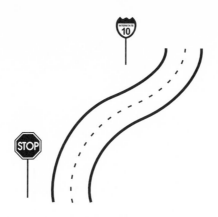

Sing-Down

A sing-down is an all-time favorite car activity. Name a category, like songs with the word "happy" in them, songs about a particular place, or songs with a person's name in the title. Challenge the kids to name as many songs as they can think of in that category. From "Happy Birthday" to "New York, New York," a sing-down will keep kids busy for miles.

Redo a Song

Have the kids in your car rewrite the words to a familiar song or musical nursery rhyme. The kids will enjoy every minute of this as they update songs like "Mary Had a Little Lamb" and "Twinkle, Twinkle, Little Star." Get ready for some serious songwriters . . . and for some silly songs.

A Grand Band

Have the children in your car pretend they are musicians and ask them to design a sound-making instrument to play in the car. They might clap their hands or snap their fingers, or they might tap a rhythm on an armrest, but all the musicians have to make a sound. Then play a song on the radio and ask them to join in. If you wish, give the children awards for the funniest instrument, the softest, the most creative, etc.

 Moving Music

Listen to a symphony or another type of classical music and ask the children to identify how the music compares to a movement they do daily. For example, the music might jump up and down, tiptoe quietly, skip lightly, or run as fast as it can. When you listen, it's almost as if you can put yourself right into the music and feel the movement.

Feel the Music

Music makes us feel different emotions. Encourage the children to listen to music and identify the feelings it evokes. Does the music sound sad, happy, or scary? Which songs make the children feel great? Which ones make them feel sad?

Road Rap

Here's a game for older children, or for children with good verbal ability. Assign each passenger a different topic, from pretzels to cats to helicopters. Challenge them to make up a rap about their topic, then take turns performing them. Here goes:

> I'm a pretzel, I'm twisted and thin,
> nobody knows the shape I'm in.
> I'm covered with salt, I have no feet,
> I'm just a snack that people like to eat.
> Yo, I'm a pretzel!

Whistle While You Ride

Have each child whistle a tune, and challenge the rest of the carpoolers to guess what song it is. The first person to guess the song correctly gets to whistle next. Some songs give themselves away with just a few notes, like "Mary Had a Little Lamb," but try harder songs that are less familiar. It might take the entire ride to guess!

Car Ride Chorus

Little ones love to sing with you as you drive the car. Invite your older passengers to sing along, too. A perfect sing-along song is "She'll Be Coming Around the Mountain." Everyone should join in, and before you know it you'll arrive at your destination with everyone feeling great.

A Mountain of Fun

Teach the children the song "She'll Be Coming Around the Mountain." Then have each player sing the song and substitute the name of his or her street for the word "mountain." Older children will eventually be able to give you all the directions for driving from their house to school. For example: "She'll be coming around Peachtree Street when she comes, she'll be taking a right turn on Lenox Road when she comes, she'll be taking a left turn on West Peachtree, then turning into our school, she'll be coming back to get us when school's out."

Disappearing Songs

Choose a short song that everyone knows, like "Happy Birthday." Have the first person sing the song and leave out the last word. The next person sings the song and leaves out the last two words. The object of the game is to continue singing until the song is no more.

Humming Home

On your ride home some day, encourage your carpoolers to try singing a song with their mouths closed—that's how to hum! Have your carpoolers choose songs and take turns humming their selections. Then ask the children to hum their songs in higher and lower voices. See which sounds the best, and let everyone help decide which hum wins.

Do-Re-Mi and You

This is a good game for learning the tones in a scale. Teach your carpoolers the song "Do-re-mi." Giving each child a turn, go around the car and let everyone sing a line from the song. The first child sings, "Do, a deer, a female deer," and the next child sings, "Re, a drop of golden sun," and so on. They'll enjoy taking turns and trying to remember what comes next—just like the von Trapp children did!

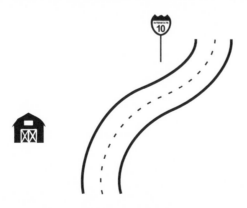

Making Music

Give each passenger a try at making up a new song that has something to do with their life. For example, if a child loves basketball, then his or her song could be about their love for the sport. If there's an artist on board, he or she could sing about their favorite form of art.

Hear me sing
Painting's my thing
I can paint most anything!

 **All That Jazz**

Introduce your riding rhythm section to jazz—one of the only musical forms born in the United States. Choose a jazz tape suitable for children. Before you know it, your hipcats in the back seat will be able to pick out the various instruments in a jazz ensemble. They might even be able to tell a tenor from a baritone sax.

 Going Global

On the way to school one morning, take your carpoolers on a trip around the world. Check your local library or music store for compilations of music from around the world. From South Africa to the British Isles, you'll be hitting the high notes on just about every continent. After listening to the different styles of music, encourage your carpoolers to guess where the music is from.

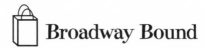 Broadway Bound

Check your local library or music store for collections of Broadway hit songs. Talk to your carpoolers about any musicals they have seen or heard about. Which were their favorites? After a few rides listening to these compilations, the children may be able to guess which song is from which musical. Before you know it, they'll be show-tune pros.

The Sound of Music

Have some fun with the song "My Favorite Things." Instruct your riders to substitute their own favorite things when they sing the lyrics. It's a great way to learn what your carpoolers really love, and, as you might have already discovered, some of your riders might not like whiskers on kittens.

 Hooray for Hollywood

Soundtracks from popular movies are a great way to pass the time in the car. Not only are they full of hit songs from films, some collections feature well-known scenes from movies. Our favorite is *The Wizard of Oz*. We all love to sing along with "Over the Rainbow," but it's fun to memorize the songs from the Cowardly Lion or the Scarecrow as well.

Leave it to Mother Nature

Music has the wonderful effect of keeping everyone calm and happy, and on some days, the sounds of Mother Nature are the perfect remedy for restless children. There are many tapes of nature sounds available, including the sounds of whales, oceans, and even rainy days. Your passengers will love the unique sounds, and you'll notice that, except for stormy weather, most of these tapes will produce a peaceful response.

Reggae to Go

Add the soothing calypso sound of a steel drum to your carpool's top ten list. Check your local library or music store for tapes of children's songs played reggae-style. Just slip the tape in, but be sure to put on your shades and "Don't Worry, Be Happy." You'll be jammin' and drivin', singing these tunes all day long.

New MacDonald

Everyone knows the song "Old MacDonald Had a Farm"—but here's a news flash. Old MacDonald moved away from the farm and into the big city. That song about him and all the cows and pigs? It's history! Encourage your carpoolers to take turns singing new verses about where Old MacDonald lives and what he's up to these days. Not only will the children love updating Old MacDonald's life, but they'll discover new and creative ways to reinvent an old standby.

Musical Bingo

Ask each passenger to name a song that is frequently played on the radio. Then turn on the radio, and see which song is played first. When someone's song is played, that person says "bingo" and scores a point. Everyone then chooses another song, or says "stick" to keep their original ones. The passenger with the most points wins.

Singing Simon Says

Create a musical version of the traditional game Simon Says. Remember, a child should do something only if Simon says to do it. If Simon doesn't say to do it, don't listen! Fun instructions include:

Sing a song as sweet as a bird.

Sing "For He's a Jolly Good Fellow" with a cat's meow.

Hum "Yankee Doodle Dandy" as fast as you can.

Bark the song "Row, Row, Row Your Boat."

Whistle "Happy Birthday to You."

Sing as low as you can.

Highs and Lows

Choose a song that everyone knows, like "Happy Birthday." Ask each passenger to try and sing the song in their highest voice and then their lowest voice. Try to do it without laughing! Let the carpool vote who has the highest and lowest voices.

Eight

Don't Flip, We're Taking a Trip
On the Road Again for Longer Trips

In case it's time to take a longer trip, get ready—if your nerves haven't been tested, this just might be your big moment. Long car trips can be exasperating. Kids and cars don't always agree, especially when kids have to sit still for long periods of time. No matter how long your trip will be, little ones and big ones alike need help dealing with the ride. The key to trips of any nature is careful planning. Here are some ideas that will help you prepare for a successful trip.

Involve the Kids

Over the years, I have learned one definite thing about traveling with kids. If your child is involved from the very start, he or she will be more inclined to cooperate. Ahead of time, read a book about your destination with your child. Make the destination come to life. If you are going to the beach, get a book about seashells. Discuss starting your own collection of shells. See how many seashells your child can name, and get prepared for the search. If a famous person lives or lived where you are headed, be sure to share historical facts about them with your child. If you're headed for Disney World, make it a small world by playing the theme song. If you're visiting Washington, D.C., bring along a book about the presidents; talk about how money is made if you plan to visit the Washington Mint. There are wonderful books about most places you will visit, and your child will enjoy knowing what to look forward to when he or she gets there.

Create a Kids on Board Kit

Help your child create a special kit to keep by his or her side during the ride. Pack up a book bag or pillowcase with favorite activities, games, stuffed animals, or books. A pillowcase works beautifully because it can double as a pillow if it's filled with soft things, and it can even serve as a laundry bag on the way home.

Create a Countdown Calendar

A few weeks before the trip, involve your child in counting down the days until you leave. You can use a ready-made calendar, and your child can cross off or place a sticker on each day as you get closer to your departure. This activity helps children measure time while building excitement about your trip. As you count down, discuss with your child things he or she can do in the car. You and your child can make a list of things to do, or write an activity on each day of the calendar as you count down.

Set a Theme

Start your trip by giving the ride a theme. Try making it a safari, a camp-out, a treasure hunt—you name it! Really get into the spirit of it. One family I know pretended they were in a boat on the ocean, on their way to a desert island. They played ABC games naming different kinds of fish, and ate cheddar goldfish for a snack. When you use your imagination, even long rides can be fun.

Prepare for Making Memories

Encourage your child to preserve his or her favorite memories and document the trip in creative ways. Begin the trip by giving each child his or her own diary and a resealable bag. Place the diary (which could just be a small notebook) in the bag, and encourage your child to store his or her favorite memories, souvenirs, etc. Your child might save a favorite rock from each stop you make, a pamphlet from the gas station about things to do and see in that area, and countless other items of choice. Odds and ends can be stored in the bag, and your child will enjoy looking at all the collected items. Encourage older children to document the trip in their diaries, recording their experiences and special facts about different areas. Younger children can draw pictures of things they see along the way.

Snips and Snails

Help each child create and maintain a scrapbook album of the journey. At the end of each day, glue or tape mementos on sheets of paper stapled together. Next to each item, have the child write a few lines about the item. If small objects (napkins, tickets, postcards, etc.) are hard to find, have the child draw a picture and write a description.

Bathroom Stops

An important rule of thumb when traveling with kids is to stop and use a bathroom, even if no one has to go. If you wait until your child says, "I need to use the bathroom," you might find yourself with a big problem. Just when you need one, a bathroom is usually miles and miles away. So don't go too far, and choose your bathrooms selectively. When you spot one that you feel will be clean and a positive experience for everyone . . . STOP!

Snacks to Pack

Snacks are an important part of a long trip, so plan them carefully. Give children a choice of healthy, non-salty snacks such as unsalted goldfish crackers, pretzels, raisins, etc. Package the snacks in resealable plastic bags or small plastic containers. Kids can eat the amount they want, then save the rest for later. Keep in mind that variety is the key, so bring small packages of assorted items. Another helpful item is a water bottle for each passenger. Chill them ahead of time in the refrigerator, and choose the bottles with the built-in tops that open and close instantly. With a permanent marker, write each passenger's name on their bottle so they won't get mixed up. Whether you plan to picnic in the car for lunch or stop at a restaurant along the way, let your child know what to expect. We've always found that stopping for lunch (even if you take it with you in the car) helps everyone, and the break does everyone a world of good. Last but not least: be sure to bring along a few small trash bags to avoid a messy ride.

Make a Shoe-Be-Do Bag

The shoe-be-do bag has been a favorite standby for us for years when traveling with our kids. Get a hanging canvas shoe bag with lots of pockets and hang it on the back of the front seat. In each pocket, put treats or snacks that your children only receive if they cooperate. The child moves from pocket to pocket as the trip continues, and by the time he or she reaches the last pocket, you're almost there! The shoe-be-do bag is full of incentives for cooperation, plus it's a great way to organize and hold a child's snacks and activities.

Make a Car Kit

Pack up a car kit with odds and ends you might need—everything from Band-Aids to wet wipes to a flashlight. Be sure to keep this kit out of the reach of young children, and bring along important information like your pediatrician's telephone number, just in case. Your car kit is for little and big emergencies, so plan carefully. With luck you'll never need it, but most trips require at least one Band-Aid.

What's in Common?

Here's a game that goes on and on, and is especially good for older kids and longer trips. Challenge your crew to think of two things that have something in common, and say them out loud. Whatever these two things have in common, however, should not be too obvious. For example, what do a telephone and music have in common? You must listen to both of them. How about a newspaper and a stop sign? They both must be read. Have kids guess what the objects have in common.

Cargo Count

Here's a fun game to play on longer trips. Each child takes a turn guessing how many passengers will be traveling in the next car you see. If the child guesses right, he or she scores that many points. The highest scorer wins!

Break the Bank

Each passenger gets a turn to be the banker and must think of an amount of money under $50. The object of the game is for the other players to guess the amount of money by asking no more than five questions. Whoever guesses the amount gets to keep the money. If no one guesses the amount, the banker can keep the money. The winner is the player with the most money at the end of the game. Players will get very creative when asking questions in this game. Instead of "Is $32 dollars in the bank?" they will quickly learn it's better to ask "Is it more than $30?"

Bigger, Smaller

Here's a game that might last forever! One player thinks of something, and everyone must guess what it is. The catch is that the players must ask if the object is bigger or smaller than another object. For example, "Is it bigger than an elephant?" The questions continue until someone guesses the object.

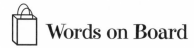 Words on Board

Write one letter of the alphabet on each of twelve index cards. Connect the cards in the bottom right-hand corner with a metal brad, so the cards spread open like a deck of playing cards. (This helps keeps the cards together and lets the kids see them easily.) Challenge your passengers to take turns making words from any of the letters on the cards. Make several sets of cards with different letters to add variety. For example, with the letters a, b, f, l, m, o, c, r, e, d, u, and s, kids might come up with bread, care, scream, more, and score.

Just Name It

Ask each player to search for objects that begin with letters of their name in order. For example, Ali might spot an airplane for A, a light for L, and an infant for I. This game can be more challenging by adding the child's name and home city. The more words, the merrier!

Silly Search

At the beginning of the trip, ask each passenger to choose something really odd to search for throughout the trip. Choices might include clowns, people with green hats on, big dogs with red collars, or anything funny and unusual. Throughout the trip, see who finds their items. You'll think you're seeing things in some of the cases, depending on what you choose.

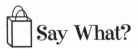 Say What?

Bring a tape recorder along and have kids tell stories and sing songs on tape, or "interview" other passengers in the car for a news or weather report. Play the tape back the next day or next hour for entertainment.

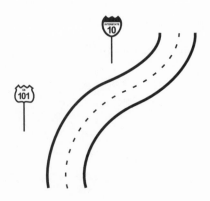

Take Note!

Don't forget to pack up plenty of tapes and music that the entire family will enjoy. Alternate interactive activities with quiet ones like listening to music. Give each family member a ten-minute turn for their music preference. Also, if possible, take a cassette player and earphones for each child and encourage quiet time. While the kids listen to their favorite music, you can pop in a recording of that book you haven't had time to read.

Car Time Can be Quality Time

Now that you've tried some of these games, hopefully you've discovered the real benefits of having fun with your kids on board. Your little ones will love the attention, and you'll love the benefits of keeping them happily occupied. Your children's minds will be turned toward something positive and productive, teaching them many new skills. As your children grow, they will also have a wealth of games and activities to choose from for instant fun and to entertain themselves and others.

I still recall a few of the games that we played on family trips when I was a child. Remember, you're not only handing down a legacy of fun and purpose, you're also giving your child special family memories that last a lifetime. And there's an added bonus! Besides increasing the smiles per hour, your children will gain and grow from the skills and learning activities that these games and activities offer.

So, whether you are driving just around the corner or forging ahead with your endless carpools and car duties, consider new ways of enjoying your kids on board and your time together. Ask your passengers what they are studying in school, then match a game to their studies, reinforcing what they are learning. Make your ride a creative one and start a carpool tradition your kids will love.

After trying a few of the games in this book, encourage each passenger to be in charge of the activity or the game of the day (give them this book for ideas). Give each child the chance to be "car captain" for the day and watch the smiles appear. Not only will they love riding in your car and appreciate your efforts, but they'll thank you for the ride every time.

Remember, as you make car time quality time, the rewards will be waiting around every corner. Not only will your passengers be more cooperative in the car and follow directions, but everyone will benefit from the smiles and meaningful time shared on board. Happy trails!

Index of Activities

Index of Activities

Kids on Board

Index of Activities